Uncommon Love Poems

By Mark Tulin

Contents

"Love is the flower of life, and blossoms unexpectedly and without law, and must be plucked where it is found and enjoyed for the brief hour of its duration." D.H. Lawrence.

This book is dedicated to those who shared their love with me.

Love's Revolution

Philadelphia held me captive,
a repeated drive down a twelve-lane boulevard,
eating hoagies every night from the Wawa market—
a city with a history, a past marriage
sliding on thin ice
and stifled by the summer's heat.

I needed a revolution,
so I manifested a west coast angel
who arrived on the wings of Spirit Airlines.

She came at the right moment,
straightened my closet of trauma,
and helped to rid me of old furniture,
attachments, and people
who no longer belong.

She replaced my stale coffee with sweet tea
and gave me a panacea for life's wrong turns.
She caressed me in her warm wings,
transported my body through barren fields,
into the citrus smells of orange groves,
and atop the mountains with snowy peaks—
healing my wounds and reviving
the passion I had lost.

The west coast angel baptized me in the salty sea
and encouraged me to model myself after the pelicans,
who soar with confidence.

Cranes of Love

Along Anacapa Street,
the birds of paradise extend
their greetings.

They are the first flowers
I notice in the morning
as I hold my cup of Joe
and venture down
a Santa Barbara road.

I give them my affection,
touch their pointed beaks,
treasure their bright colors,
and exchange pleasantries
like close friends.

They speak in a tropical tongue,
attracting the sunbirds
to pollinate their goodwill,
nourished by the ocean mist,
an occasional sprinkle,
and the music of the sun.

O cranes of love,
gentle is your garden,
in harmony with your surroundings,
flower in your noble bloom,
reminding me to stop and behold.

Sunburnt Bride

In this desert theatre,
I wait for you in tattered clothes,
bloodied by the broken glass,
writing love letters in the wind.

We will celebrate our bond
under a wooden bridge
among friends who toss old shoes
to celebrate our fertility.

You will be my sunburnt bride
in a succulent garden
with the snakes and coyotes
as our bridesmaids for an eternity.

O, my blooming succulent,
my demon in the night,
the flesh binds us
in the sands of nomadic life.

Light us up, O God of fiery hope,
consummate our marriage,
and sanctify our charred desire—
let us live among the rocks
until the vultures
pick our bones.

High School Emotions

High school heartbreak
was my most painful loss.
Its wounds ran deep
in my adolescent spirit;
the scars never disappeared.

I walked out of class
the day she shunned me,
sneaking past the hall monitor;
self-pity was my closest ally,
her new boyfriend, my adversary.

Eyes of the moon.
Hair as dark as a raven in the night.
I kept questioning myself,
why does losing a love feel so bad?
Rejection hurts more than the truth.

The alluring siren sang her song.
If only I could see her again;
maybe if I wait long enough,
she'll knock on my door,
or send me a letter
with her perfume.

I realize now she was an illusion,
a figment of a boy's imagination,
but desire suppresses reason
when high school emotions
have no soft place to land.

Like a D.H. Lawrence Love Poem

The sensual softness of trumpet petals,
its brightness and simplicity,
nature's yearning for color,
most vividly alive.

Its long slender stamen,
a lighthouse for nectar-seeking birds—
red, white, and yellow,
a China rose,

Hawaiian and tropical,
a gentle garden mallow
blooming in the heart's eye—
it flowers then fades.

But while she blooms,
she is the wonder of creation
within a stolen moment—
love must be admired
wherever it is found.

Love must be enjoyed,
said D.H. Lawrence—
no matter how brief its duration.

Is it not so?

Bumper Car Angel

I loved the bumper-car angel
in her silver and red vehicle.
She was crazy beautiful,
a maniac behind the wheel,
unafraid to collide
with a Sunday driver
or a kid twice her size.

I tailgated her,
ignoring friends
who tried to rock me
out of my insanity
with a fender bender
and a head-on slam.

My bumper car angel
drove like a mini Danica Patrick,
static electricity everywhere,
love sparks, making my heart
jump start.

A lovestruck boy
sideswiped a long-haired girl,
but my advances were ignored;
instead, she depressed
the pedal and disappeared
at lightning speed.

Love can blindside you.
It can go fast or slow
or take sharp turns.

Sometimes it feels like
a passionate embrace
when force meets energy;
other times, a chance opportunity
that goes awry.

Racing after you,
I was in a bumper car dream,
a million screams,
a collision course that ended
once the power went off.

You hopped out and ran
to your parents' waiting arms
while I drowned my sorrows
in a triple-decker ice cream cone
and a ticket to the pirate ship ride.

Sensual Rain

Clouds dimmed the candlelit skies
A woman veiled by the shadowy moon
Deep brown skin and hair dripping from rainwater
Her mysterious eyes as big as saucers

She was a rainstorm happenstance
She stole my heart in the sensual rain
Together, we crossed the universe
The steamy ocean flowed through us in waves

Our clothes fell like falling fronds
Desire warmed our naked bodies
Passion shook us with a shivering lust
Our embrace molded in the sea of time

A fleeting romance with no regrets
A sad ending to a blissful sunrise
Fate had brought our souls together
Love's bittersweet moment had torn us apart.

The Dancehall

I wish to thank the universe
for providing me
with a good dance partner
to a Gershwin or an Ellington tune,
a waltz, or a swing.

Although we stumble
and step on each other's toes,
we somehow move
about the dance floor
without harming anyone.

Our technique is simple,
unlike Rogers and Astaire,
an Irving Berlin cheek-to-cheek,
slow and mindful
with a bend and twirl.

Our confidence is high,
and coordination is maintained.
We are conscious of our spirit;
dancing is not about what you know
but about sharing what you've learned.

Sometimes I take the lead;
other times, I defer,
but together, we are equal,
vulnerable yet strong,
hopeful yet cautious.

I keep the rhythm
while my partner tangos on the floor.
The universe is the choreographer,
and under the stars and moon,
the dancehall.

My Poetry Muse

My poetry muse visits daily,
often coming to me in dreams
in the middle of the night
when I can't fall asleep.

I see her on a country road,
through farm towns
with omens and hex signs,
and during long walks
on mountaintops
by the edge of the cliffs.

Her voice is resonant,
like Mama Cass
or a howling feral cat.
She is a kindly muse,
a bit on the wild side,
who compels me to scratch and claw
until I finish my thought.

She is a divine reverie,
a welcome creative
whose free-spirited song
drives my iambic pentameter.

Please, write from the gut
with poetic defiance—
verse *with a romantic bent*
but far-fetched and irreverent.

My muse guides my poetry,
a whisper that lights fires,

and encourages me
to conspire with the angels
and break bread with the devil.

Love's Transcendence

My sweet flower is much more
than her family and friends.

More valuable to me
than the books she reads,
the gifts she gives,
and the lines she remembers
from my poetry.

She is more than a molecular
collection,
more potent than an energy field.

Her radiant bloom
grows more beautiful
with each midday sun.

A woman I wouldn't trade
or alter,
whom I see with the heart's eye.

Pure and loyal,
as trustworthy as the stars.

Our connection cycles
through life and death
and endless reincarnations.

Our bond transcends
any measure of time.

Love's Intertwine

She is the light
He is the shadow
Inseparable
Nature's balance
Formed through each
Movement
Through art's intermingle
Her essence
His skill

The model drops her robe
She flows into position
And holds the pose
Breathing barely audible
As the emerging artist
Embraces her design
A relationship is formed
In a silent room

Eyes never meet
Lines curve and cross
Love's intertwine
By soft and eager hands
Charcoal shading
Against twilight's canvas
Spatial partners in time
The artist at the easel
The model in recline.

The First Date

From a first date
to a wide-eyed joyride,
down the question-and-answer lane,
inside a surreal ice cream shop
full of funhouse mirrors,
two people staring at their reflections.

We lost track of time,
transfixed on the
creamy coldness
of our youthful innocence,
seeing how far we'd go,
how close we'd come—

barely remembered our names,
tongues circling pretzel cones,
lapping love's sweetness,
catching rainbow sprinkles,
and random giggles,
falling from the sky,

a spiral of soft-serve swirling,
attention-seeking, yearning
as the ice cream slowly melts
like sugary waterfalls,
strawberry and vanilla
droplets on the floor.

A Poem in My Shirt Pocket

Thank you, Sara,
for the poem
I carry
in my shirt pocket.

It comforts me
that you are only as far
as your words are close.

Your presence
is in the ink of your pen;
your heartbeat
in the rhythm of your verse.

Each line
spills softly over the page
like the smoothness of your face,
the cursive of your body.

Each stanza
that ends in a period
stands wistfully alone
in the metaphor of your memory.

An Ancient River

A lonely woman lives in a corner duplex,
surrounded by untrimmed green hedges;
an easterly breeze occasionally blows
from an ancient river.

In the spring, she plants tomatoes,
patiently waiting for them to ripen,
picking each gently from the stem,
and cradles a half-dozen in her apron.

In the summer, she sits on a folding chair
with her legs dipped in a kiddie pool,
a pool of motherhood to be remembered
where the waves of painful memories
ebb and flow.

She imagines her son as a boy,
splashing in the shallow water,
sailing his wind-up motorboat,
his eyes green and hair a light brown,
his youthful skin is glistening from the sun.

As she dips her toes into the freshwater,
under a little beach umbrella,
she sadly smiles at a lifetime of sorrow—
a stillborn child, she will never know.

Jazzy Jiggy Love

There's no dance I want to do
than the dance of improvisation,
spreading my limbs wide,
cutting the cake,
moving under a jive sun
in the colors of the mind,
showering my little head
with silly musical notes.

There's no sensation I want to feel
than the exhilaration of the moment,
the fragrant early morning,
the sounds of the pitch-black night,
and lazy country afternoons
where I rock myself to sleep
on a hammock between two jiggy trees.

There's no universe I want to breathe in
than the one I swing in now—
the jazzy tunes I want to play
on my saxophone of love,
the pounding beat of a tom-tom,
and fingers sliding across the piano keys.

Homemade Moments

I'll miss my home
when I die;
the stickies stuck to the wall
with my ideas,
computers charged on power cords,
and palm trees swaying to wind music
outside my window.

I'll miss the brown sofa
I shared with my wife,
watching baseball games
and old black-and-white movies
starring Clark Gable and Spencer Tracy.
They don't make stars like that
anymore.

I must have cooked a thousand stir-fries
on our old black wok,
chopping onions and carrots
and adding the baby bok choy
to our savory mix.

There will be no more hand drums
played in the living room,
the beating of my conga
and the tapping of my bongo
will stay quiet in storage.

No longer will smoke rise
from the metal teapot,
the blueberry hibiscus bag

dropped into the cup,
or my wife's warm hand in mine
during tender moments.

Special Occasion

I know it's true love
because you are here with me
during my last breath.
You are the only one I want
to share it with
on this special occasion.

It doesn't bother me
that you remember
how I looked
when I was younger,
or how weak
I am now.

With you, I am not scared
or vulnerable,
but feel safe to let go.
You allow me to leave
on my terms
without remorse or fear.

In my final expiration,
your presence
is a holy comfort,
a warm shroud,
and a shining light
for my new journey.

Growing Together

We are both flowers on a summer day
Growing together from fertile soil
Absorbing the effervescent sun
Birds drifting in levitation
Souls rooted in fields of green
Our delicate petals open and curve
Expanding outward with the universe
Bees buzzing innocently around us
Hummingbirds drinking our nectar
All of nature approves of us
We are in harmony with the earth
Celebrating our love in the morning
Amidst the reds, purples, and golds.

Double Pneumonia

My love is chronic,
affecting both body and mind;
an emergency room visit
and a bed in intensive care.

Love gives me
double pneumonia.
You kiss the lips that turn white
and have no compassion
for my suffering.

Then you take
the color from my face
and make my temperature rise.
Then transform the joy of life
into a lovesick sallow,
a hacking cough,
and a pauper's demise.

From your lethal beauty
to your X-ray eyes,
you steal my breath,
fibrillate my heart,
and leave me love-ridden
for more.

Yellow Flower

I see you in a yellow flower
growing from the fertile soil,
soft as a hibiscus petal,
as delicate as a stem,
blooming at the right moment,
awakening a beauty within.

I see you in a yellow flower,
the universe's colorful smile,
cooling as summer rain,
vibrant as the morning sun,
fragrant as first love,
sleeping under a crescent moon.

Our Love is in Hardcover

I pick up a copy of our love story
in a new hardback edition,
making sure the dust cover is intact.
I gently open the pages,
discovering our truth in each line,
the paragraphs of our romance,
lives that are freshly bound,
and turn each page carefully
so as not to crinkle or bend.

I caress the sturdy spine,
plant a kiss on the endpaper,
tasting your bold typeface lips,
saying I love you in Garamond print,
savoring our themes, our plot—
beginning, middle, and end,
and promise I'll never read
or so much as look at
another softcover edition again.

Jose's Lover

Jose had not been with a woman
except for the one he slept with.
The one the aide had to inflate
with a hand pump and muscle.

There was no one like her,
an hourglass figure,
an endearing movie starlet,
beautiful, realistic, and plastic.

They worked well at night
with his mangled limbs
and her silent, frozen look
without breathing or movement.

He wished that one day
he'd turn into a prince,
and she would wake up
just like a Disney fairytale.

And then they could make love
as non-disabled people do,
with the window shades open
under the stars and full moon.

Awkward Adolescent Words

Sometimes maudlin verse
can be nauseating,
the spilling of romantic feelings
splattered on the page.

Sometimes, a poet must write
about love's cliché in rhythm,
tenderly and self-indulgent
with much sentimentality.

Sometimes the soul has to express
its overly emotional heart
in awkward adolescent words,
not so subtle or refined.

Sometimes a poet has to get
down on his metaphorical knees
and humble himself
in the name of sappy love.

An Early Bird Special

We put down our blankets
and watched the sunrise.
I passed the popcorn,
and my wife spilled candy
into my open palm.

It was the early bird special,
surrounded by the pigeons
and seagulls, surfers
waxing their boards,
and early morning tugboat horns.

The spectacle was in technicolor,
in surround sound,
awe-inspiring,
nature's love story,
as the sun rose so effortlessly.

The film had plenty of drama,
well-directed, expertly produced,
and a good-supporting cast—
it's the ultimate moving picture
with a bit of avian humor.

We were on the edge of our seats,
watching every moment
as the darkness slowly brightened
with the excitement of a new morning.

The hero was the sun,
who saved the day just in time,

while the moon was shown
during a later performance.

When the movie was over,
we gave it a standing ovation;
an Oscar-worthy performance,
and stayed until the credits rolled
like clouds across the sky.

Blackbird Love

Blackbird love,
wire-hanging,
lamppost pecking,
like island lovers
unafraid of public displays
of affection.

Blackbird love,
beak to beak,
wing over wing,
sunrise dreaming
of exotic feasting
to crawdaddy melodies.

Blackbird love
in a Garden of Eden,
a mercurial paradise,
sensual spaces,
clouds swirling
in a surrealistic sky.

Blackbird love
soon to fly
low and smooth
over a winding dirt road
past lush greens and palm trees
to the edge of heaven.

The Perfect Place

My mother died, but don't worry,
she's all right, doing just fine;
she spends her days in a wooden box
with me, sleeping on the grass outside.

She's calm—doesn't say a word,
eat a thing, or move an inch;
nothing seems to hurt, plenty of fresh air,
warm sunshine, and cool nights.

She's where she wants to be,
the perfect place to reside,
with her son by her side
deep in the woods.

Ashes burnt from the past,
memories drifting in the sea,
no longer flesh and achy bones,
no longer cataracts and hammertoes.

Blue Collar Angel

Dad woke me at 2 a.m.
It was hard to leave a warm bed
and a bubblegum-flavored dream.
"It's time for us to go to work," Dad said,
"to buy fruit and vegetables for our store."

It was bitterly cold outside.
The winds rattled the double-pane windows,
and the snow came down
hard and heavy
over the darkened houses of our street.

But I could not refuse.
Dad was my blue-collar angel
who told me to wear long johns
and a heavy coat with a fleece-lined hood.
"And don't forget your galoshes," he reminded.

So, I wiped the crust from my eyes
and left the comfort of the woolen blanket
as we made our way decisively
through the slushy streets of Philadelphia
into the soul of an unforgiving winter,
where the two of us broke the morning silence.

Throw and Chase

I remember tossing the red ball
into the tumbling waves,
and my dog retrieved it
with his paws paddling.
It seemed that time slowed,
and we never tired,
but kept our game going
in an endless succession.

Throw and chase was our ritual,
a man-dog brotherhood,
our way of staying connected,
sharing the sun-splattered instant
when the morning felt fresh forever,
and the waves never ceased to entertain.

But as the seasons passed,
we eventually grew old,
and my dog developed a bad hip.
I inherited my mother's cataracts
and my eyes were too blurry
to play in the bright sunshine.

We became two aging comrades
who preferred the quiet of a living room.
I leaned back in the lounger,
my dog curled by my feet
on a rug near a space heater,
while I nostalgically remembered
how my dog was excited by the chase,
and I was more than happy to throw.

Calla Lilies

She paints in a quiet corner
of a coffeehouse,
destined to dip her brush
into a small tub of water,
and dab it into an array of pastels
onto a small white canvas
and paint calla lilies
in watercolor.

She paints for her friends,
her lovers, the world's beauty,
the treasures to be seen,
the gardens to be planted,
and the memories to be saved.

She paints in gentle strokes,
taking her time around curves,
like a woman's figure,
long green stems,
a yellow center,
moon-colored petals
ready to flower
by soft, knowing hands.

Painted Stones

The spirits breathed life
into the hand-painted stones
of Ventura's spiritual garden,

colorful heart-shaped rocks,
symbols of lost loved ones
who once roamed the beaches,
made footprints in the wet sand,
and inhaled the seaside air.

Now they are faces
etched in dreams,
memories in pictures,
and tears to be recovered
in frozen moments.

They lost their lives
for different reasons,
leaving wives and husbands,
sons and daughters
for distant stars
and uncharted adventures.

In this garden of spirits,
memories turn from sadness
into youthful laughter
as the seabirds fly
over the crashing waves
in an aerial salute.

Raindrops

Sipping on a sea
of brewed coffee
with sleepy eyes,
I look out the window
when it rains
at an angled view
of beads of moisture
gently streaming
in a shadowy room
where it's just me
and the sound
of raindrops
tapping.

You Share So Much

Your love is your creamy, soft skin.
Kindness, your forgiving heart.
Thoughtfulness, your open arms
that soothes a greedy soul
on the days when I want too much.

Your love is in the way
you heal my brokenness
with bedtime kisses
and patient moments
when you hold your tongue
at my thoughtless words.

You share so much
and give all of yourself to me
even when I don't deserve it.
I only wish you had enough love
left over for yourself.

Tuna Breath

Grandma cranked the old-fashioned opener,
making sure not to touch the sharp edges
of the Chicken of the Sea can.

The tuna juice floated to the top
like algae from the ocean.
She wondered what fisherman
fished them out.

With her arthritic fingers,
she chopped the tuna
like her mother taught her,
mixing hard-boiled eggs and onions
and adding plenty of salad dressing.

She cried every time she cut an onion.
The nitroglycerin pill rested carefully
beneath her tongue
so her heartbeat could stop thumping
in unsteady rhythms.

She smiled through the pain
as her two cats rubbed against her,
lining up to lick her fingers
and waiting patiently for a taste.

They looked up at Grandma,
hoping she'd share some juice from the can,
while breathing in her tuna breath.

Mary in the Garden

Mary stands near the fountain,
a white statue of dignity and love,
for squirrels to climb,
the crows and blue jays to perch,
a quiet shelter for the silence of the night.

The rose bush rubs against her face,
fragrant with thorns and petals.
She feels the California sunshine,
an occasional coastal breeze
that plays softly like backyard music.

Mother Mary is in my imagination,
a part of my everlasting soul.
She has always meant more
than the cement and resin
that stands patiently with open hands
to receive our blessings.

Oak Park in the Afternoon

Old trees have wisdom, bent over
like aging prophets preaching.
The crows say I have arrived for a new
beginning and point me in the right direction.
The fragrance of lavender wafts
through the air, reviving my waning spirit.

I go to Oak Park each afternoon
to transform my rigid soul into softness,
rediscovering forgotten parts of myself.

I walk barefoot on the green grass,
watch celebrations, mariachi bands playing
shiny brass instruments, grandmothers doting
over their young grandchildren,
and piñatas smashed into a million pieces.

The sun's warmth heals my old wounds;
good friends slip into slow Tai Chi moves,
as a teenager balances on a tightrope
to inspire me to try new things.

The landscape stops me
from thinking a negative thought.
Instead, my mind wanders
to the scent of the orange groves,
the rows of Sequoia trees,
and the mountains in the distance.

It is a California park where families grow,
romances are born, secrets are shared,

and an ocean so close,
you could hear the waves break.
And when a cool breeze touches my face,
I know nature has taken care of me.

A Sensual Reflection

The instant your image
catches my eye,
there's a vision of satisfaction,
a shy new beginning,
a fantasy playing with my imagination.

My chest heaves with desire,
the look when our eyes meet;
then euphoria sets in,
and I'm lost in anticipation.

I'm compelled to reach out,
to touch one finger,
then another,
until reason and passion
collide and explode
without knowing the direction.

And when my nakedness meets yours,
it's as dizzying as a merry-go-round
until the spinning ride is over,
and I hold you
in the stationary pool
of reflection
when I can't return
to the moment before.

Watching Candles Burn

I know my mother's here
by her presence
in the white candle
that burns on the sink
in the kitchen.

I know she hovers
by how the red glow
flickers
in the shadows.

She always loved
watching the flames
of Yahrzeit candles
slowly burning wax
to the bottom of the glass.

It made her feel
not so lost
and deserted
by the family
who left her behind.

Even in death,
she still needs
a burning white candle
to keep her spirit
from flickering out.

Lifeguard Aphrodite

My lifeguard beauty,
my Aphrodite,
sits upon her metal throne,
a lifeguard station
to watch over us,
bronzed by the California sun.

I long for her Baywatch body
to rescue me with love's grip
in a one-piece Speedo bathing suit,
in a flash of a courageous moment.

To save me from the Great White,
to blow her silver whistle
when I'm stuck in an undertow
and deliver me
from my childish crush
before I hit the jagged rocks.

Love Letter to Alice

To my naked mango blossom
The woman who shares my queen-size bed
A sweet coconut drink
A candy coated with milk chocolate
A marine layer, soft and transparent
The sunrise that wakes me up
The cozy moonlight at sleep

You are my native Tahitian
The beauty that Gauguin painted
Without you, I'd be lost
An artist without an easel
You rescued me from a harsh winter
A stowaway to Santa Barbara
A wedding night in Las Vegas
The marital knot tied by King Elvis

My brown-eyed, sun-splashed fruit
My pearl at the bottom of the sea
My grand grandiosity
My sprinkled, sparkled ice cream cone
My goddess, my princess, my majesty
My fantasy came to life
My wife, my wife, my wife.

Sympathy to Spare

We were random strangers
whose paths crossed
at a CVS parking lot.
She had lost a good friend,
and if I would be so kind
as to lend her my shoulder.

She wanted a solid body to hug,
whose heart was still beating,
and who had sympathy to spare.
She thanked me when it was over
and vanished down the road,
past the bank and the ice cream parlor.

She walked by a church with a steeple
into the hustle-bustle of our everyday lives
where someone's pain touches another
and whose caring gesture
comforts our wounds.

The Art of Helping

I push her wheelchair
to the dollar store,
navigating the bumps in the road,
changing her dressing
that hides an open sore,
and careful that the alcohol
doesn't burn.

I cook her meals
from a recipe book,
low in fat and salt.
My hands blend in love
with a woman whose joy
is also my healthy fare.

Helping, I do with great desire,
to embrace a neglected soul
whose smile opens wide
despite the pain in her jaw,
often too difficult to bear.

I read her a bedtime story
about a blind woman
who miraculously sees,
and before she closes her eyes,
I prop her head,
covering her feet and arms
so she doesn't catch a chill.

I turn off the lights each night
in recognition of this honor;
to aid a disabled woman
with a benevolent attitude
is my reward, not a burden.

Horn of Compassion

A frail older woman in a wheelchair
Squeezing, humming out notes
Through a long skinny bone
Each vibrating sound awakens us
Calls us to stand and listen
With gratitude and sympathy
With respect and courage
She blows the horn of compassion
For the rich and poor
For the healthy and infirm
With all the air in her fragile lungs
She blows the didgeridoo
For everyone.

His Last Vignette

My father loved the smell of beer,
the salty stale pretzels,
and the pigs' feet floating in a jar.

He loved the neighborhood saloon,
small-town men with fat bellies
and balding heads, telling of their salvation
while serving in the war.

My father loved the freedom of the stool,
the way it turned but never spun off.
He loved his Mom and Pop tattoos,
and his crooked jaw,
broken during the Korean War.

He told of the time,
he almost married a French woman
that he gifted with a bar of soap
and a pair of stockings
he bought at the commissary.

His romance in the service
ran its unhappy course
when my father got homesick
for his dear old mother
and an American cheeseburger.

The barflies were so impressed
at how my father held his liquor,

such a hard worker, a stand-up guy,
and a damn good storyteller.

As my father told his last vignette,
he put down his drink,
and took a drag of a Lucky Strike,
as the ceiling fan circled
his immortalized youth.

Aunt Marion

When I was a kid, Aunt Marion
read me seashore stories
about the giant whale
who swallowed Jonah,
and the elusive Moby Dick
that Captain Ahab couldn't catch.

Together, we washed clean our troubles
with each curling rush
and held hands tightly,
our heads above the breakers
and paddled from the undercurrent
to the safety of the beach.

We watched scary movies in the dark
on her fuzzy Sony Trinitron
and ate popcorn and Cheese Doodles
as the sharks circled us in dangerous waters;
and when Frankenstein roamed the countryside,
Aunt Marion protected me.

A California Street

I had a dream when I was nine,
living by the California coast,
walking down a wide street,
past palm trees, roses of all colors,
and Spanish-style houses with fountains.

I fell in love with the warm sun,
the clearness of the turquoise sea,
the smell of the salty air,
and how beautiful paradise must be.

When I woke from the dream,
I was no longer by the ocean,
but walking along a broken path,
down a tree-less Philadelphia street
with row homes and abandoned cars.

The sky was a murky gray.
The air was foul.
Only the faint breeze from the Delaware
reminded me of the Pacific.

Love's a Dog

Love bites when you're not looking,
licks your face
when you're stretched on the sofa—
and you shouldn't take it for granted
no matter how messy it gets,
'cause love is not permanent—
the love songs
will testify to that,
it comes and goes
like the Santa Ana winds.
It puts you on top of the world,
and just like that,
you're blown from its pedestal,
breaking into a million pieces,
'cause you're not hard-boiled,
no one is—
but you wish you would have tried harder,
but it wouldn't have mattered—
fate and love are tied together,
in one slippery ball of wax,
'cause you can't teach it, train it,
or make it stay—no,
you can never control love.
Still, you can be nice to it
when it's here.

The Summer of Love

Whatever happened to the Age of Aquarius
when love ruled the land,
when hippies walked barefoot,
let it all hang down, wore tie-dyes,
groovy peace sign medallions
and worshiped Mother Earth.

Whatever happened to 1967
when being rich didn't matter;
Sunday was a toke in the park,
hair frizzy and long, love-ins,
and spontaneous poetry readings
on the streets of Haight-Ashbury.

Whatever happened to the flower children
who bloomed on grassy summers
like psychedelic mushrooms sprouting,
and whose wide eyes were full of hope,
breathing in youthful innocence,
playing love songs on a folk guitar.

Tree of Dreams

Once we plant a tree,
it becomes a dream.
We dig the soil of our future,
nurture the fledgling daily,
and watch it gradually take shape,
enabled by the sun and rain.

We plant with good intentions
and care meticulously for the sapling,
like tending to a newborn,
enabling it to blossom
with a gardener's love
as it tells its own story.

We watch the tree take root
and, over the years, spread out
its full canopy
and anchor itself
deep within the ground,
absorbing Mother Earth
as its primal source.

The tree softens the harsher
elements of life—
a refuge for sojourners
and transients seeking shade.
The tree becomes our legacy,
a gift on public display,
quietly changing lives.

The Wooden Urn of Memories

In your honor,
I set free your earthly remains
from the wooden urn of memories,
so your fate can guide you
in your journey
for lasting peace.

I release you into the moving waters,
the swirls of your destiny,
where there is no sin
or religion to restrain you,
no public opinions
to alienate you from others.

You are now wiped clean
of all your human flaws,
the misery of the past,
and scattered to the sea
with your ancestors
and spirit guides.

Return to the water, dear Mother,
from where you have risen,
the vast vista of promises,
the coral reds and oranges,
so you can alter your shape,
regenerate your soul
and resume the cycle of samsara.

Venice Beach Mermaid

The homeless man on the beach
sculpted the woman of his dreams
with gnarled hands and a kid's shovel.
He may have been destitute and hungry,
but he had the passion of Michelangelo.

He carved her sandy flesh
into smoothed edges,
serrated her fishtail,
and gave her life
by the magic of the sun.

A mermaid! He exclaimed—
sensual and slender,
able to provide hours of friendship,
to share stories by the sea,
and ease his loneliness.

Her quiet presence, he enjoyed
until the tide was high
and his only faithful companion
melted by a wave,
along with his heart.

The Day We Drove to Vegas

I remember that March morning
when we had *huevos rancheros* with Uncle Pete
and drove the California and Nevada highways
to matrimony in Las Vegas.

We played Spanish tunes on the radio
for your parents in the backseat,
who reminisced about their wedding day
at a quiet little church in Santa Paula.

We passed dusty deserts along the way,
broken down gas stations, abandoned shacks,
the berry stands off the asphalt roads,
and Joshua trees huddled together in full bloom.

I remember seeing you smile
when you thought it would never be you
to find such a loving man
in the breath of the sacred angels.

We went down long winding roads,
driving hundreds of miles on low-octane,
straight through until we hit the jackpot,
the Lucky Little Chapel.

It was located at an outdoor mall
with a praying mantis sculpture
and a thousand locks made of hearts,
and the manager said when we arrived late,
"I thought you had changed your mind."

It all came from an online game of Scrabble,
me from the East and you from the West;
words and fate had brought us together,
despite much resistance
from friends, family, and coworkers.

Many thought it was too big of a gamble.
But we trusted our intuitions
as the casino wheels spun
and found ourselves at the precipice
of a new life in our middle years.

I stood on a quarter next to the pastor,
waiting for you to float down the aisle
with your proud Mexican father
as Elvis sang, "Blue Hawaii."

I broke your grandmother's wine glass.
You married into a Hebrew tribe,
far removed from the Aztec ruins
you rose from.

At night, the full moon hung over us
and seemed to sing from the balcony
as we cradled our future together,
sleeping on fine silk sheets.

When the wedding day ended,
we returned to our coastal town,
taking our honeymoon on the sand—
with one REI chair for you
and the other for me.

California Love

California is an alluring beauty,
swaying hips on rollerblades,
streaks of sunlight across her face,
and salty kisses of ocean mist.

Her fragrance, freshly-picked strawberries,
and the citrus of orange groves.
Her beauty is a field of golden poppies
and mustard grass growing on the hillsides.

She speaks through barking elephant seals
and screeching seagulls,
Monterey's cool sea breeze
and the Mojave's windswept colors.

She flies over canyons and mountaintops,
soaring like Icarus toward the sun,
and rises like a surfer queen
slicing through a seventy-foot Maverick wave.

Teach Me Things Other Than Love

"Marry me so I can teach you to live and teach me to die."
—Charlie Chaplin to Oona O'Neill.

Relationships aren't all about romance.
The attraction is more practical
than kissing or holding hands—
It's about teaching each other
how to live and how to die,
and feeling more secure in our skins.

Couples have the answers,
if only we asked for what we wanted,
come together in good faith,
share truths about love and death,
and accept each other's fates.

Freedom was my gift to give.
I taught my wife how to disengage,
and not be bound and indebted
by the closeness of friends and family.

And she taught me
how to live out a dream—
find a space to write poetry
with truth and hope.

I opened her mind,
while she opened the windows.

We both let in some fresh air,
organized our pasts,
listened to our hearts,
and allowed our destinies to follow.

Acknowledgments

Age of Empathy: "The Art of Helping"
Amethyst Review: "Blue Collar Angel"
Blue Insights: "An Early Bird Special" "Blackbird Love"
Breathe Bold: "Painted Stones"
Disquiet Arts: "Sunburnt Bride"
Duane's PoeTree: "Special Occasion"
Elephant Journal: "On the Road to Vegas"
Gardening, Birding, and Outdoor Adventure: "Cranes of Love"
Illumination: "Love's Transcendence"
Literary Yard: "Double Pneumonia"
Luna: "Raindrops"
Move Me Poetry: "High School Emotions" "The Wooden Urn of Memories"
Poetic Essences: "Teach Me Things Other Than Love"
Red Wolf Editions: "Growing Together" "Venice Beach Mermaid"
Sensual, An Erotic Life: "Sensual Rain" "Love's Intertwine"
Spillwords: "A Poem in My Shirt Pocket" "Awkward Adolescent Words" "The Perfect Place" "Calla Lilies" "Mary in the Garden" "Watching Candles Burn" "Sympathy to Spare"
The Lark: "Oak Park in the Afternoon"
The Rye Whiskey Review: "The Last Vignette"
Truth Serum Press, Verdant Issue: "Ancient River"
Visitant: "A California Street"
Visual Verse: "Jazzy Jiggy Love"
Weeds and Wildflowers: "Like a D.H. Lawrence Love Poem"

Cover image by Mark Tulin.
Author's picture by Erica Urech.

About the Author

Mark Tulin is a former family therapist from Philadelphia who lives in Long Beach, California, with his wife, Alice. He is a Pushcart Prize nominee, a Best of Drabble, a Glimmer Train honorable mention, and runner-up in The Lark Poetry Competition. A poetry publisher once compared Mark's poetry to artist Edward Hopper on how he grasps unusual aspects of people's lives. "I want my words to reflect my soulful essence—proving to me and others that I once roamed this planet." Mark's books include *Magical Yogis, Awkward Grace, The Asthmatic Kid and Other Stories, Junkyard Souls,* and *Rain on Cabrillo,* available at Amazon.com. Mark has appeared in Story Radio, Haight Ashbury Literary Journal, Amethyst Review, The Drabble, Page and Spine, Fiction on the Web, Vita Brevis Press, Remington Review, The Literary Hatchet, Spillwords, The Writing Disorder, Red Wolf Editions, New Readers Magazine, Still Point Arts Quarterly, and many anthologies and podcasts. Follow Mark at http://crowonthewire.com.

www.ingramcontent.com/pod-product-compliance
Lightning Source LLC
Chambersburg PA
CBHW051818130726

47987CB00003B/1306